2ND EDITION

PIANO · VOCAL · GUITAR

THE BEST LATIN SONGS EVER

LATIN

ISBN 978-0-7935-8934-0

HAL•LEONARD®
CORPORATION

7777 W. BLUEMOUND RD. P.O. BOX 13819 MILWAUKEE, WI 53213

Visit Hal Leonard Online at
www.halleonard.com

CONTENTS

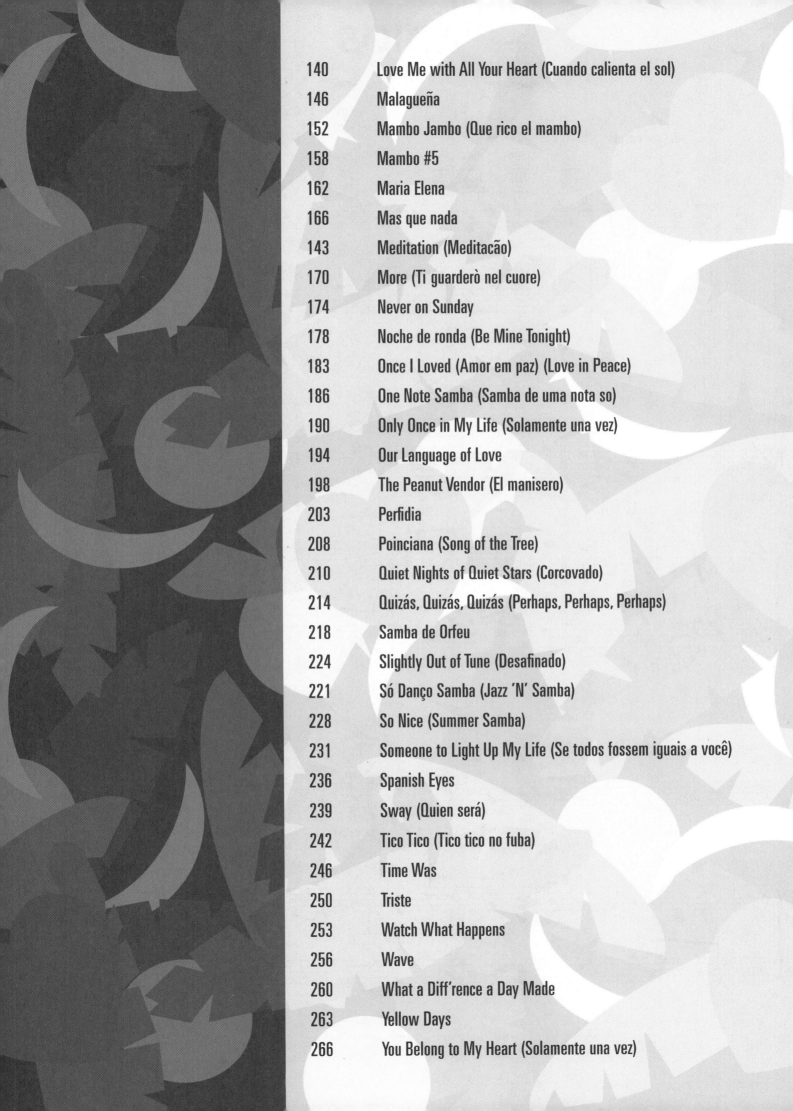

ADIOS

English Words by EDDIE WOODS
Spanish Translation and Music by ENRIC MADRIGUERA

Moderately

We were so hap-py, dear, _ to-geth er, _ and ev i-'ry dream of joy _ we knew. _
Ya la a-le-grí-a de _ mi vi-da _ es co-mo un sue-ño que _ se va _

_ A cas-tle in the air, _ dear, for-ev - er, _ a world of love for just _ we two.
_ por-que al lle-gar de nue-vo el dí-a _ con mi i-lu-sión me he de a-le-jar _

AMAPOLA
(Pretty Little Poppy)

By JOSEPH M. LACALLE
New English Words by ALBERT GAMSE

heav - en - ly. _____ Since I found you, _____

____ my heart is wrapped a - round you, _____ and lov - ing you, it

seems to beat a rhap - so - dy. _____

____ A - ma - po - la, _____ the pret - ty lit - tle

ALWAYS IN MY HEART
(Siempre en mi corazón)

English Lyric by KIM GANNON
Original Words and Music by ERNESTO LECUONA

AMOR
(Amor, Amor, Amor)

Music by GABRIEL RUIZ
Spanish Words by RICARDO LÓPEZ MÉNDEZ
English Words by NORMAN NEWELL

ANEMA E CORE
(With All My Heart)

English Lyric by MANN CURTIS and HARRY AKST
Italian Lyric by TITO MANLIO
Music by SALVE d'ESPOSITO

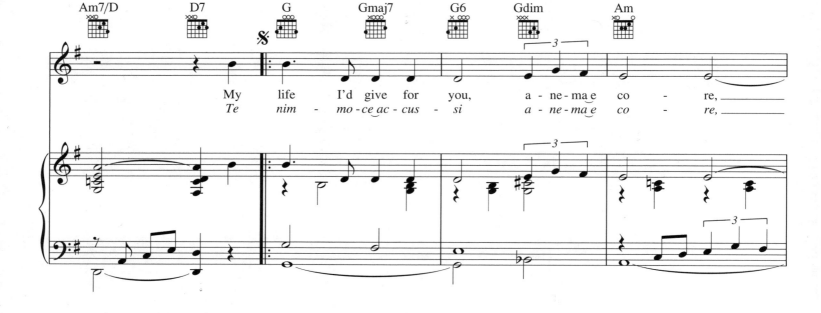

My life I'd give for you, a-ne-ma e co - re,
Te nim - mo-ce ac-cus - si a-ne-ma e co - re,

I on - ly live for you, a-ne-ma e co - re.
Nun nce las-sam-mo cchiú, man-co pe' n'o - ra

AQUELLOS OJOS VERDES
(Green Eyes)

Music by NILO MENENDEZ
Spanish Words by ADOLFO UTRERA
English Words by E. RIVERA and E. WOODS

Life held no charm, dear, un-til I met you. _____
Fue - ron tus o - jos los que me die - rón _____

BABALÚ

Words and Music by
MARGARITA LECUONA

BÉSAME MUCHO
(Kiss Me Much)

Music and Spanish Words by CONSUELO VELÁZQUEZ
English Words by SUNNY SKYLAR

Bé - sa - me, _____ bé - sa - me mu - cho, _____

Bé - sa - me, _____ bé - sa - me mu - cho, _____

each time I cling to your kiss I hear mu - sic di - vine. _____

co - mo si fue - ra es - ta no - che la úl - ti - ma vez;

Bé - sa - me mu - cho, _____

bé - sa - me mu - cho, _____

BESAME MUCHO 1940 by Mexican songwriter Consuelo Velazquez

(Writing the song at approx. 15 years old Consuelo claims she had not yet been kissed.....though the title translates, "Kiss Me Much")   **Arrangement: Bobby Tomei**   TN Cinco De Mayo 2011

(INTRO)   Dm //// A7 //// Dm //// A7 ////

Dm   Gm
Be-sa-me, besame   mu - cho,
                 F#dim   Gm   A7   Dm// A7// Dm////
Each time I   cling to your   kiss, I hear   music di - vine,
D7   Gm
Be - sa -me, besame   mu - cho,
Dm   A7+5   A7   Dm//// ////
Hold me my darling and   say that you'll   always be   mine.

Gm   Dm
This joy is something new,   my arms enfolding you,
A7   Dm
Never knew this thrill be - fore.
Gm   Dm
Whoever thought I'll be   holding you close to me,
E7   A7
Whisp'ring "It's you I a - dore."

Dm   Gm
Dearest one, if you should   leave me,
                 F#dim   Gm   A7   Dm// A7// Dm////
Each little   dream would take   wing and my   life would be   through,
D7   Gm
Be - sa - me, besame   mu - cho,
Dm   A7+5   A7   (To Top) Dm//// ////
Love me forever and   make all my   dreams   come   true.
                                              (End) Dm//
                                    A7// Dm// Gm// Dm// A7// Dm//// /

BESAME MUCHO

1940 by Mexican songwriter Consuelo Velázquez

CUANTO LE GUSTA

Original Words and Music by GABRIEL RUIZ
English Words by RAY GILBERT

BLAME IT ON THE BOSSA NOVA

Words and Music by BARRY MANN
and CYNTHIA WEIL

BRAZIL

Original Words and Music by ARY BARROSO
English Lyrics by S.K. RUSSELL

THE BREEZE AND I

Words by AL STILLMAN
Music by ERNESTO LECUONA

CHEGA DE SAUDADE
(No More Blues)

English Lyric by JON HENDRICKS and JESSIE CAVANAUGH
Original Text by VINICIUS DE MORAES
Music by ANTONIO CARLOS JOBIM

CUMANÁ

Words by HAROLD SPINA and ROC HILLMAN
Music by BARCLAY ALLEN

A DAY IN THE LIFE OF A FOOL
(Manhã de carnaval)

Words by CARL SIGMAN
Music by LUIZ BONFA

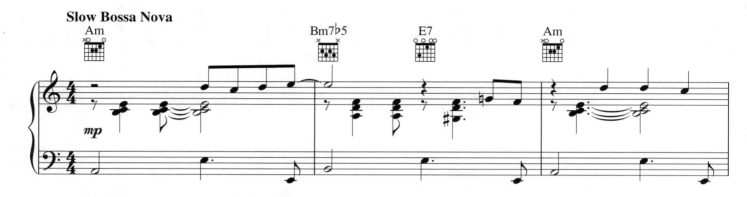

Slow Bossa Nova

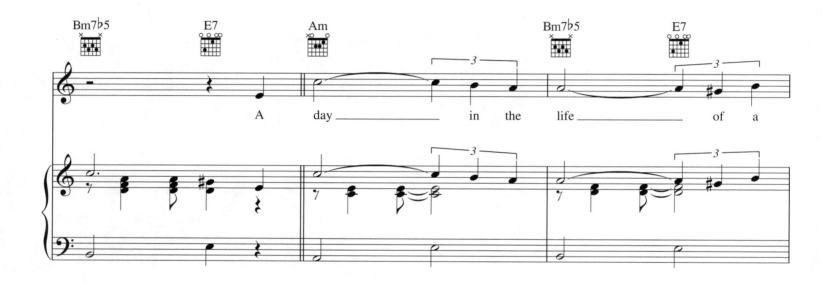

A day ___ in the life ___ of a

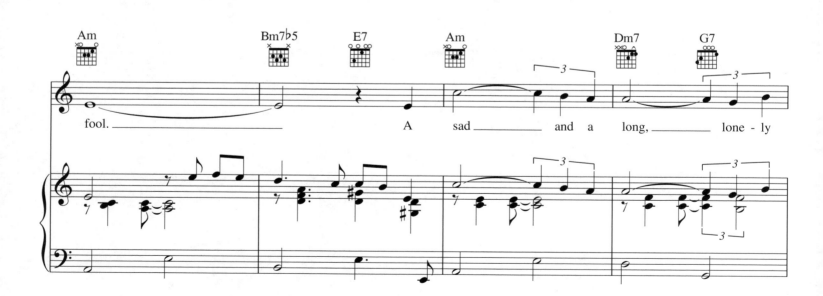

fool. ___ A sad ___ and a long, ___ lone-ly

THE END OF A LOVE AFFAIR

Words and Music by
EDWARD C. REDDING

Moderate Beguine

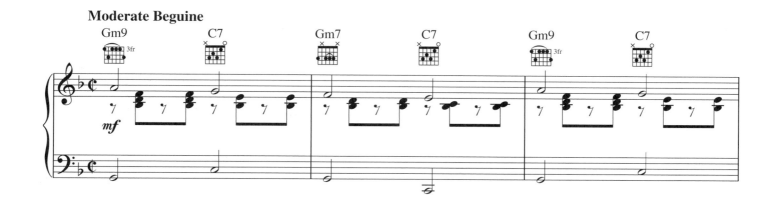

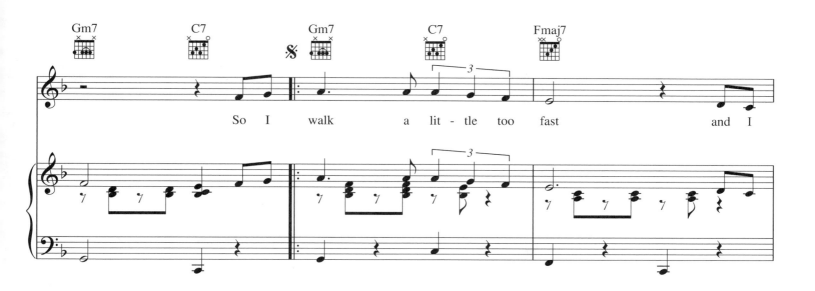

So I walk a lit - tle too fast and I

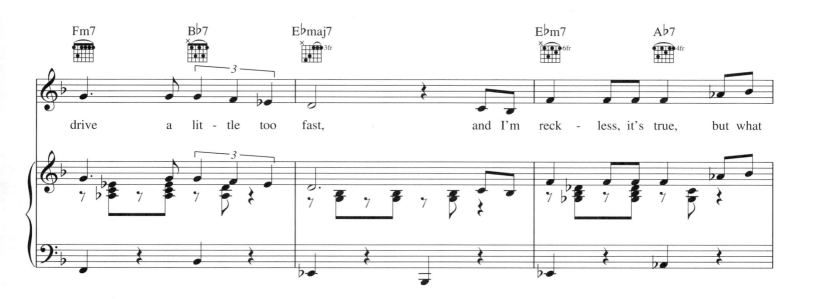

drive a lit - tle too fast, and I'm reck - less, it's true, but what

DINDI

Music by ANTONIO CARLOS JOBIM
Portuguese Lyrics by ALOYSIO DE OLIVEIRA
English Lyrics by RAY GILBERT

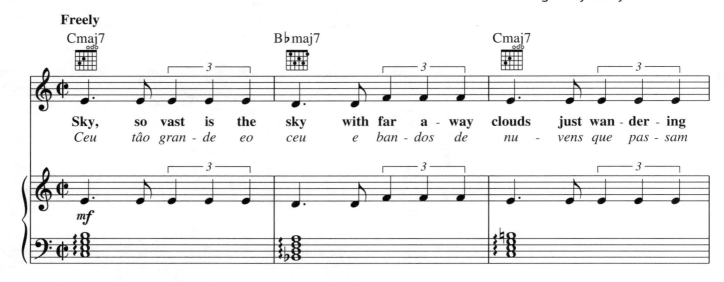

Sky, so vast is the sky with far a-way clouds just wan-der-ing
Ceu tâo gran-de eo ceu e ban-dos de nu-vens que pas-sam

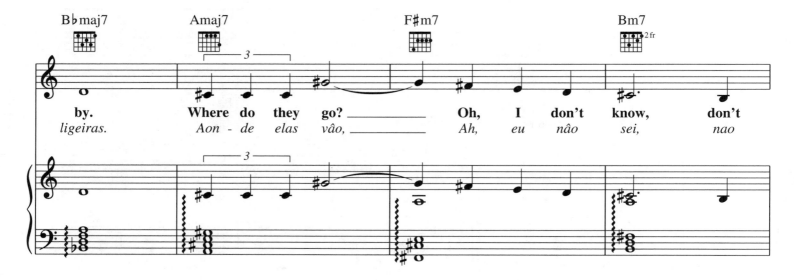

by. Where do they go? _____ Oh, I don't know, don't
ligeiras. Aon-de elas vâo, _____ Ah, eu nâo sei, nao

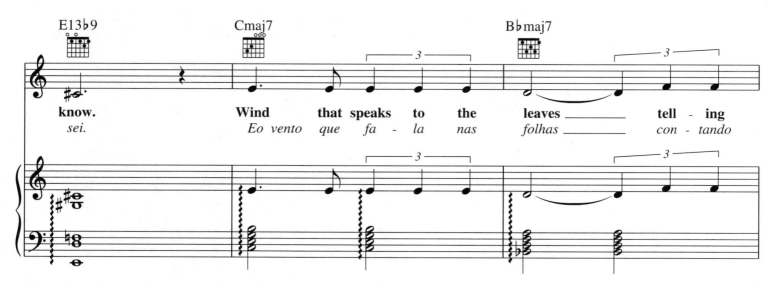

know. Wind that speaks to the leaves _____ tell-ing
sei. Eo vento que fa-la nas folhas _____ con-tando

76

DON'T CRY FOR ME ARGENTINA
from EVITA

Words by TIM RICE
Music by ANDREW LLOYD WEBBER

all you have to do is look at me to know that ev - 'ry word is true.

FLAMINGO

Lyric by ED ANDERSON
Music by TED GROUYA

The white clouds hang from the sky a- bove _____ and my love has gone a-

way. _____ Oh ex- o- tic bird pas- sing

o- ver- head lis- ten to what I say: Fla-

THE FOOL ON THE HILL

Words and Music by JOHN LENNON
and PAUL McCARTNEY

Day af-ter day, a-lone on a hill, ___ The
Well on the way, head in a cloud, ___ The

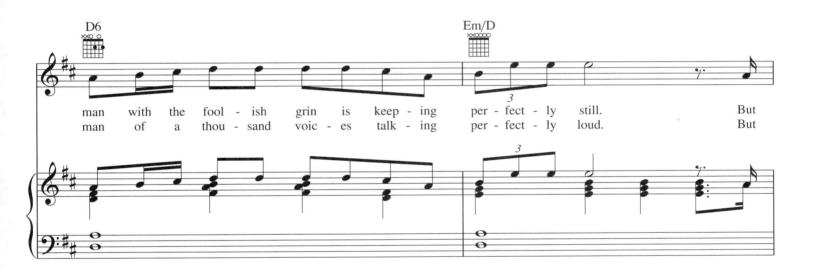

man with the fool-ish grin is keep-ing per-fect-ly still. But
man of a thou-sand voic-es talk-ing per-fect-ly loud. But

no-bod-y wants to know ___ him, They can see that he's just ___ a fool. ___ And
no-bod-y ev-er hears ___ him, Or the sound he ap-pears ___ to make. ___ And

FRENESÍ

Words and Music by
ALBERTO DOMÍNGUEZ

94

GRANADA

Spanish Words and Music by AGUSTÍN LARA
English Words by DOROTHY DODD

THE GIFT!
(Recado bossa nova)

Music by DJALMA FERREIRA
Original Lyric by LUIZ ANTONIO
English Lyric by PAUL FRANCIS WEBSTER

THE GIRL FROM IPANEMA
(Garôta de Ipanema)

Music by ANTONIO CARLOS JOBIM
English Words by NORMAN GIMBEL
Original Words by VINICIUS DE MORAES

GUADALAJARA

Words and Music by
PEPE GUIZAR

GUANTANAMERA

Musical Adaptation by PETE SEEGER and JULIAN ORBON
Lyric Adaptation by JULIAN ORBON, based on a poem by JOSE MARTI
Lyric Editor: HECTOR ANGULO
Original Music and Lyrics by JOSE FERNANDEZ DIAZ

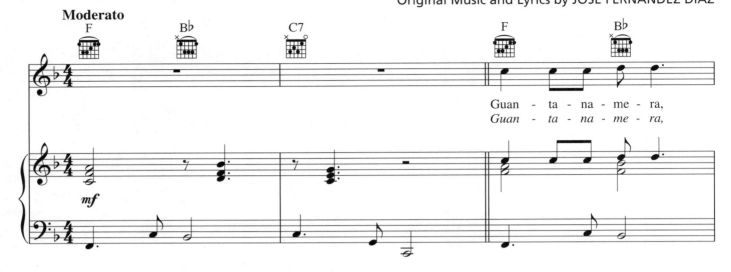

114

Additional Spanish Lyrics

2. Mi verso es de un verde claro,
Y de un carmin encendido,
Mi verso es un ciervo herido,
Que busca en el monte amparo.
Chorus

3. Con los pobres de la tierra,
Quiero yo mi suerte echar,
El arroyo de la sierra,
Me complace mas que el mar.
Chorus

Additional English Lyrics

2. *I write my rhymes with no learning,*
And yet with truth they are burning,
But is the world waiting for them?
Or will they all just ignore them?
Have I a poet's illusion,
A dream to die in seclusion?
Chorus

3. *A little brook on a mountain,*
The cooling spray of a fountain
Arouse in me an emotion,
More than the vast boundless ocean,
For there's a wealth beyond measure
In little things that we treasure.
Chorus (in Spanish)

I GET IDEAS

Words by DORCAS COCHRAN
Music by JULIO C. SANDERS

HOW INSENSITIVE
(Insensatez)

Music by ANTONIO CARLOS JOBIM
Original Words by VINICIUS DE MORAES
English Words by NORMAN GIMBEL

How _____ in - sen - si - tive _____
Now _____ {he's} {she's} gone a - way, _____

___ I must have seemed _____ when {he} {she} told me that ___ {he} {she} loved ___ me.
___ and I'm a - lone _____ with the mem-'ry of ___ {his} {her} last ___ look. _____

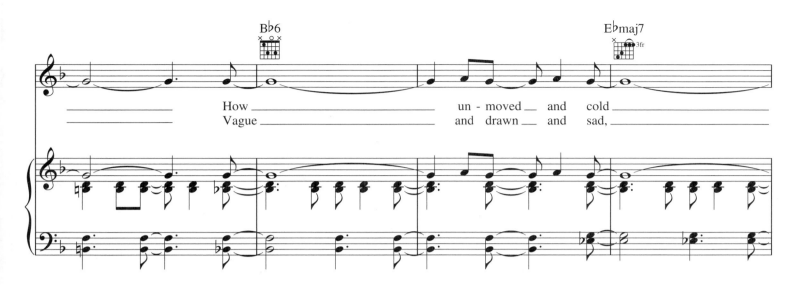

How _____ un - moved ___ and cold _____
Vague _____ and drawn ___ and sad, _____

___ I must ___ have seemed ___ when {he}{she} told me so ___ sin - cere-
___ I see ___ it still, ___ all {his}{her} heart-break in ___ that last ___

- ly. _____ Why, _____
___ look. _____ How, _____

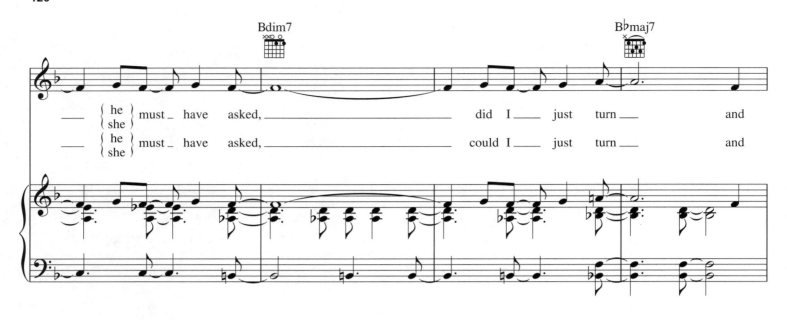

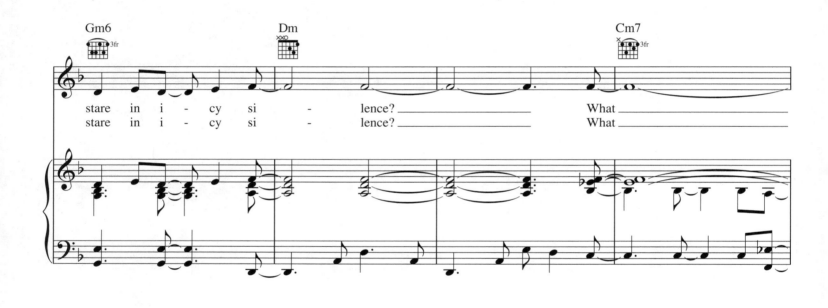

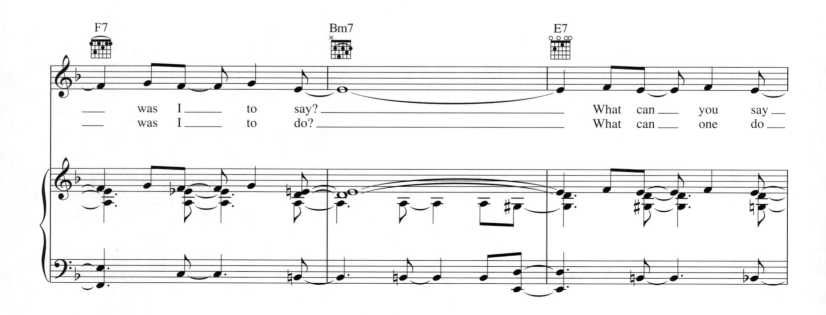

Portuguese Lyrics

*A insensatez
Que você fez
Coração mais sem cuidado
Fez chorar de dôr
O seu amôr
Um amôr tão delicado
Ah! Porque você
Foi fraco assim
Assim tão desalmado
Ah! Meu coração
Que nunca amou
Não merece ser amado
Vai meu coração
Ouve a razão
Usa só sinceridade
Quem semeia vento
Diz a razão
Colhe tempestade
Vai meu coração
Pede perdão
Perdão apaixonado
Vai porque
Quem não
Pede perdão
Não é nunca perdoado.*

INOLVIDABLE

Words and Music by
JULIO GUTIERREZ

IT'S IMPOSSIBLE
(Somos novios)

English Lyric by SID WAYNE
Spanish Words and Music by
ARMANDO MANZANERO

It's im-pos-si-ble, tell the
So-mos no-vios pues los

sun to leave the sky, it's just im-pos-si-ble.
dos sen-ti-mos mu tuo a-mor pro-fun-do.

It's im-pos-si-ble, ask a
Y con e-so ya ga-

128

KISS OF FIRE

Words and Music by LESTER ALLEN
and ROBERT HILL
(Adapted from A.G. VILLOLDO)

THE LOOK OF LOVE
from CASINO ROYALE

Words by HAL DAVID
Music by BURT BACHARACH

Dm7(add4)   D7sus   D7   Bb6

of love, ____   it's say - ing so ___
to - night, ____   let this be just __

Bbm6   Fmaj7   F7

__ much more __ than just words could ev - er say. _____
__ the start __ of so man - y nights __ like this. _____

Bbmaj7   Bb6   A7sus   A7

And what my heart __ has heard, _ well, it takes my breath __ a - way. __
Let's take a lov - er's vow __ and then seal it with __ a kiss. __

Dm7   G7   F   Gm7/C

__ I can hard - ly wait to hold you, feel ___ my arms a - round you, **6/4**

LITTLE BOAT

Original Words by RONALDO BOSCOLI
English Words by BUDDY KAYE
Music by ROBERTO MENESCAL

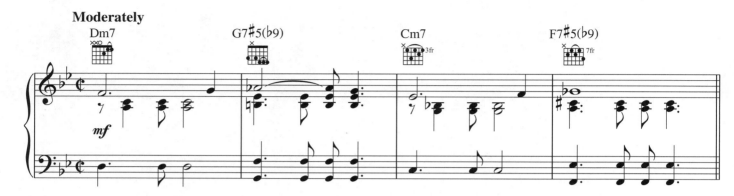

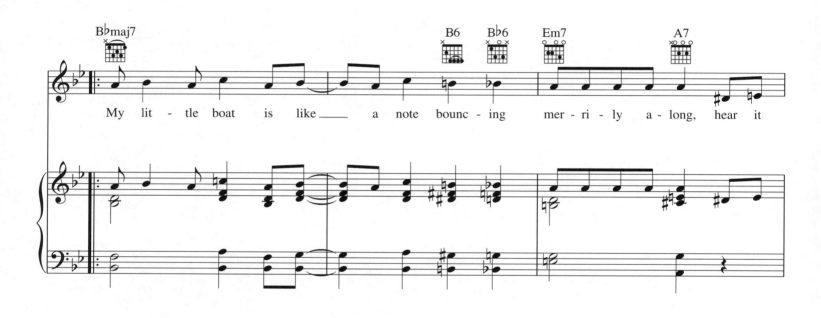

My lit-tle boat is like ____ a note bounc-ing mer-ri-ly a-long, hear it

splash-ing up a song. The sails are white, the sky ____ is bright head-ing

LOVE ME WITH ALL YOUR HEART
(Cuando calienta el sol)

Original Words and Music by CARLOS RIGUAL
and CARLOS A. MARTINOLI
English Words by SUNNY SKYLAR

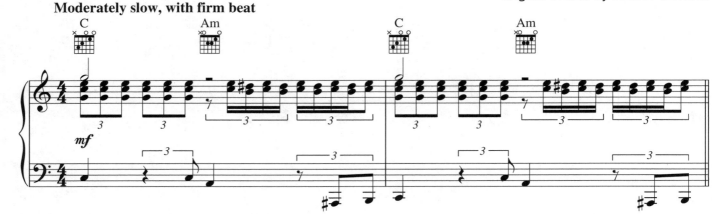

Love me with all your heart, __ that's all I want, love; ____
Cuan - do ca - lien - ta el sol ____ *a - quí en la pla - ya,* ____

Love me with all of your heart or not at all; ____
sien - to tu cuer - po vi - brar cer - ca de mí,

MEDITATION
(Meditacão)

Music by ANTONIO CARLOS JOBIM
Original Words by NEWTON MENDONÇA
English Words by NORMAN GIMBEL

MALAGUEÑA
from the Spanish Suite ANDALUCIA

Music and Spanish lyric by ERNESTO LECUONA
English lyric by MARIAN BANKS

Ah, _____ ah.
Ah _____ *Ah* _____

"Fly a - way!" said my care - free heart, "to the place where the day - dreams
El a - mor me lle - va ha - cia ti con im - pul - so a - rre - ba - ta a-

Moderately fast Flamenco

(1.) My Ma - la - gue - ña, your eyes shamed the pur - ple sky.____
(2.) Long have I trav - eled, my love, since the night we met,____
(1.,2.) Ma - la - gue - ña de o - jos ne - gros,____

You were as fair as I dreamed you would be.____
seek - ing in wan-d'ring a way to for - get.____
Ma - la - gue - ña de mis sue - ños.____

stream, I   fol - low   in   a   dream. _____

ni - ta   te   quie - ro   be - sar. _____

D.S. al Coda

CODA

heart. _____

rer. _____

poco a poco accel.

MAMBO JAMBO
(Que rico el mambo)

English Words by RAYMOND KARL and CHARLIE TOWNE
Original Words and Music by DAMASO PEREZ PRADO

MAMBO #5

Words and Music by
DAMASO PEREZ PRADO

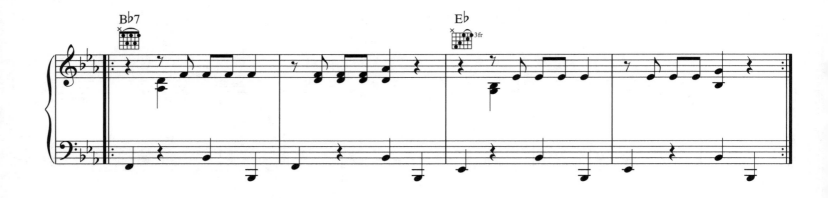

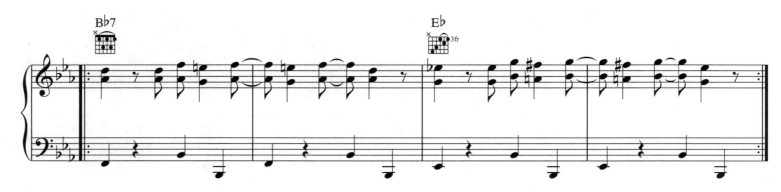

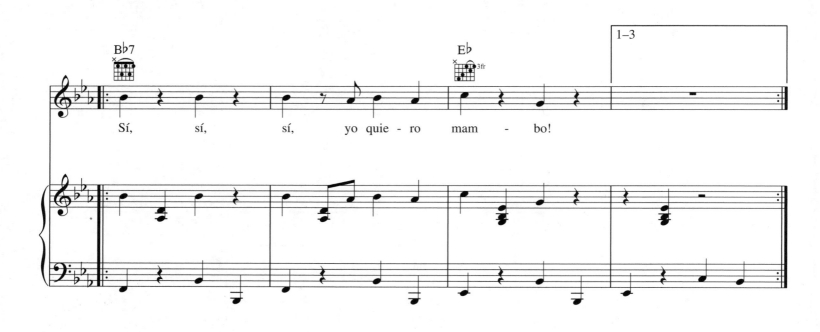

Sí,   sí,   sí,   yo quie - ro mam - bo!

MARIA ELENA

English Lyrics by S.K. RUSSELL
Music and Spanish Lyrics by LORENZO BARCELATA

MAS QUE NADA

Words and Music by
JORGE BEN

Moderado rápido

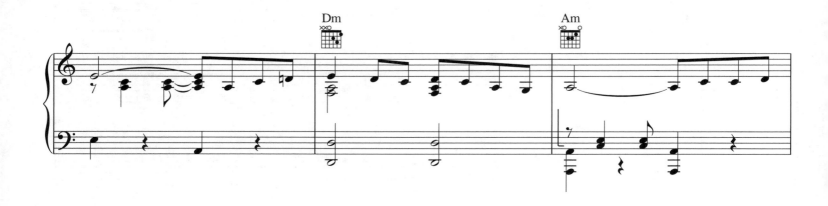

MORE
(Ti guarderò nel cuore)
from the Film MONDO CANE

Music by NINO OLIVIERO and RIZ ORTOLANI
Italian Lyrics by MARCELLO CIORCIOLINI
English Lyrics by NORMAN NEWELL

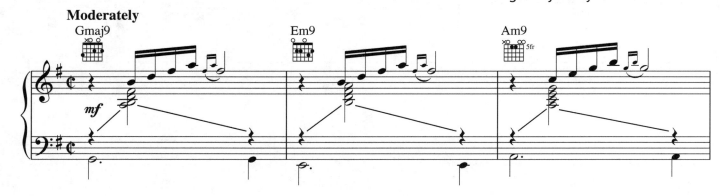

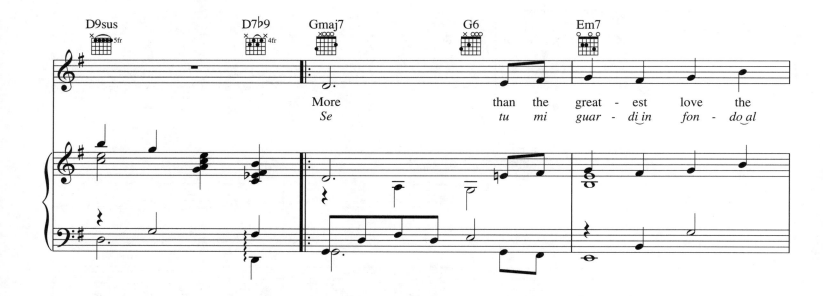

More than the greatest love the
Se tu mi guar-di in fon-do al

world has known; this is the
cuor, ve-drai Un no-me

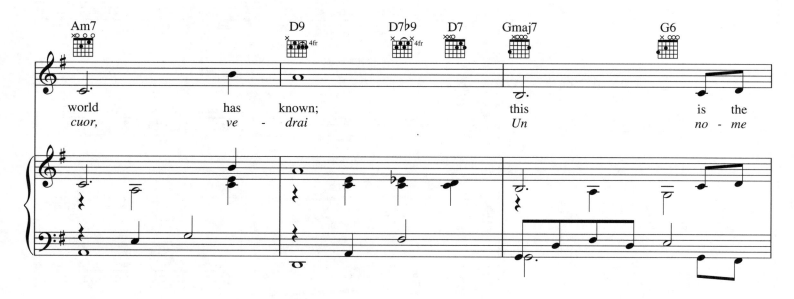

NEVER ON SUNDAY

from Jules Dassin's Motion Picture NEVER ON SUNDAY

Words by BILLY TOWNE
Music by MANOS HADJIDAKIS

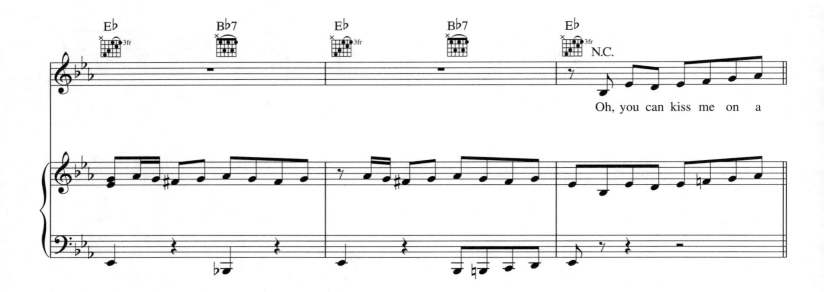

Oh, you can kiss me on a

Mon - day, a Mon - day, a Mon - day is ver - y, ver - y good.
cool day, a hot day, a wet day, which - ev - er one you choose.

NOCHE DE RONDA
(Be Mine Tonight)

Original Words and Music by MARIA TERESA LARA
English Words by SUNNY SKYLAR

* English lyrics skip to next asterisk.

ONCE I LOVED
(Amor em paz)
(Love in Peace)

Music by ANTONIO CARLOS JOBIM
Portuguese Lyrics by VINICIUS DE MORAES
English Lyrics by RAY GILBERT

Bb9#5
Ebmaj7
Eb6
I cried at the
I know that no
Em7b5
Eb9#11
1
Dmaj7
thought. I was fool - ish and proud and let you say good - bye.
mat - ter what - ev - er be - falls, I'll nev - er
D7#5
2
Dmaj7
G7
let you go. I will hold you close.
Cmaj7
F13
Bbmaj7
Make you stay.
3fr
5fr

Portuguese Lyrics

Eu amei, e amei ai de mim muito mais do que devia amar.
E chorei ao sentir que eu iria sofrer e me desesperar.

Foi antão, que da minha infinita triztesa aconteceu você.
Encontrei, em você a razão de viver e de amar em paz
E não sofrer mais. Nunca mais.
Porque o amor é a coisa mais triste quando se desfaz.
O amor é a coisa mais triste quando se desfaz.

ONE NOTE SAMBA
(Samba de uma nota so)

Original Lyrics by NEWTON MENDONCA
English Lyrics by ANTONIO CARLOS JOBIM
Music by ANTONIO CARLOS JOBIM

Lightly, with movement

ONLY ONCE IN MY LIFE
(Solamente Una Vez)

Music and Spanish Words by AGUSTÍN LARA
English Words by RICK CARNES and JANIS CARNES

E♭ E♭6 Edim7
life, to love com -
más se en - tre - ga el
B♭7 N.C. Fm
plete - ly; spend the rest of my life
al - ma, con la dul - ce y to - tal
Fm7 B♭+ E♭ E♭maj7
with on - ly you.
re - nun - cia - ción
E♭ E♭6 E♭maj7 E♭6 E♭maj7 Edim7
In a prayer or a dream to be - lieve that love could last for -
y cuan - do e - se mi - la - gro rea - li - za el pro - di - gio de a -

OUR LANGUAGE OF LOVE

from IRMA LA DOUCE

Music by MARGUERITE MONNOT
Original French words by ALEXANDRE BREFFORT
English words by JULIAN MORE, DAVID HENEKER and MONTY NORMAN

THE PEANUT VENDOR
(El manisero)

English Words by MARION SUNSHINE and L. WOLFE GILBERT
Music and Spanish Words by MOISES SIMONS

In Cu - ba, each mer - ry maid wakes up with
In Cu - ba, his smil - ing face is wel - come

this ser - e - nade: "Pea - nuts! _____ They're nice ___ and hot.
most ev - 'ry place. "Pea - nuts!" _____ they hear ___ him cry.

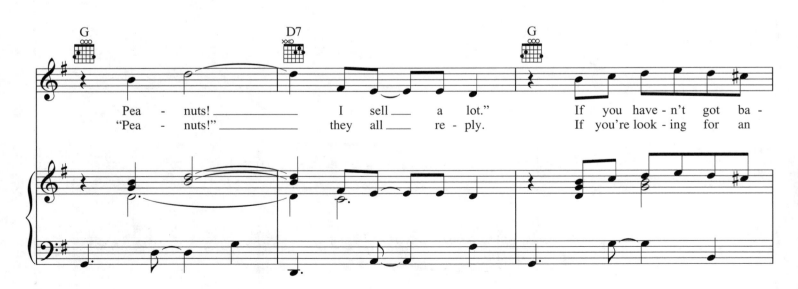

Pea - nuts! _____ I sell ___ a lot." If you have - n't got ba -
"Pea - nuts!" _____ they all ___ re - ply. If you're look - ing for an

PERFIDIA

Words and Music by
ALBERTO DOMÍNGUEZ

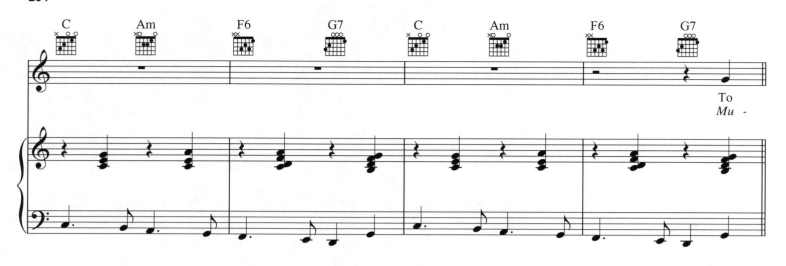

To
Mu -

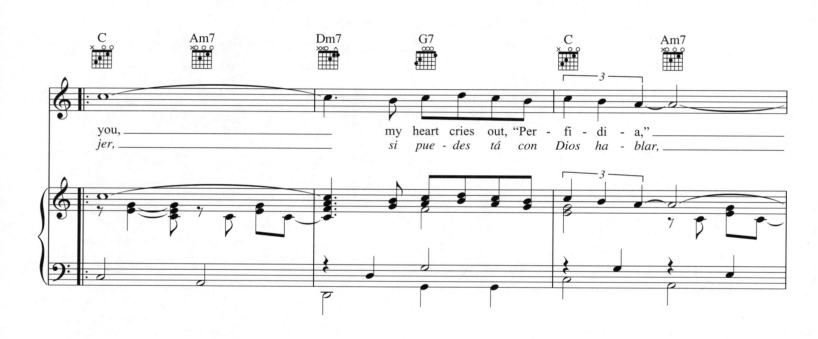

you, _____ my heart cries out, "Per - fi - di - a," _____
jer, _____ si pue - des tá con Dios ha - blar, _____

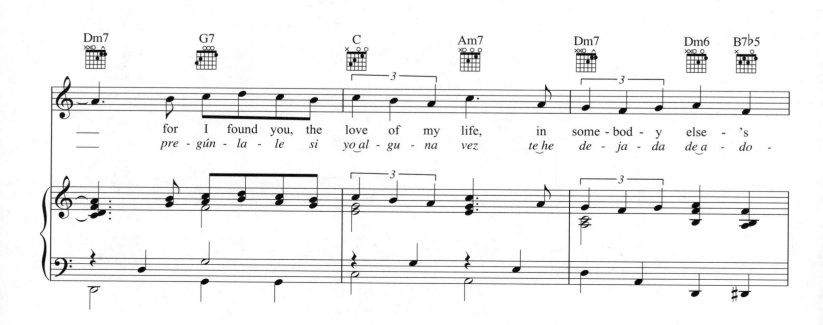

for I found you, the love of my life, in some - bod - y else - 's
pre - gún - la - le si yo al - gu - na vez te he de - ja - da de a - do -

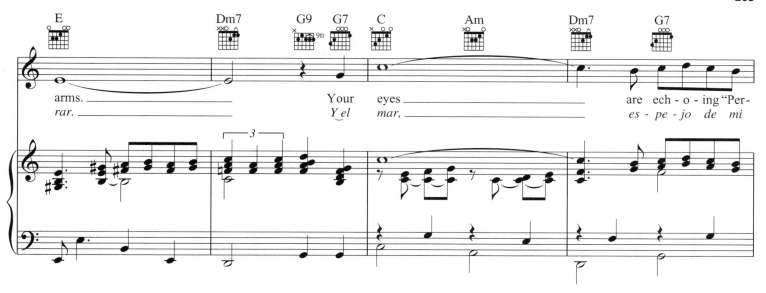

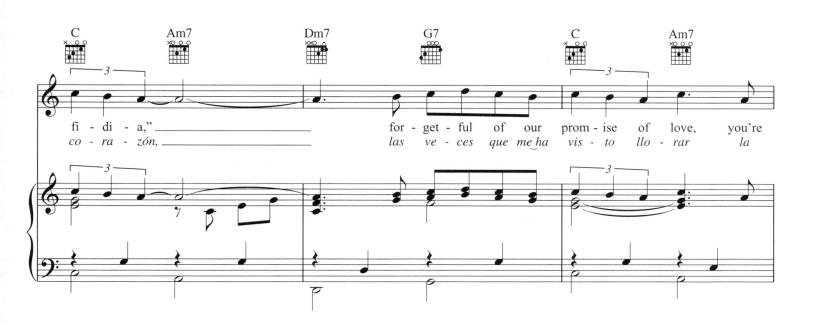

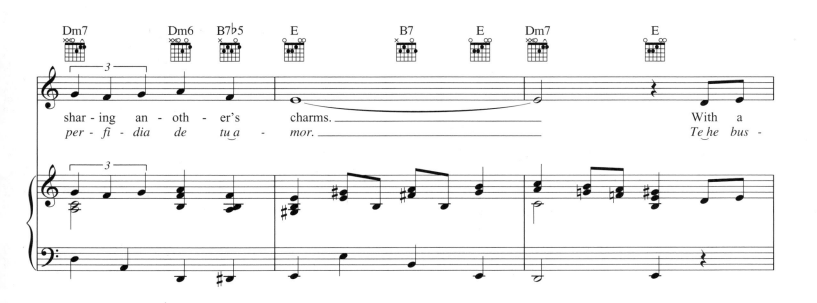

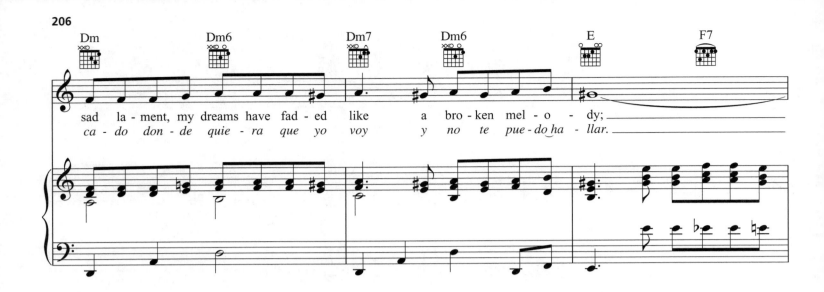

sad la - ment, my dreams have fad - ed like a bro - ken mel - o - dy; _____
ca - do don - de quie - ra que yo voy y no te pue - do_ha - llar. _____

_____ While the gods of love look down and laugh at what ro - man - tic fools we mor - tals
_____ ¿Pa - ra qué quie - ro_o - tros be - sos si tus la - bios no me quie - ren ya be -

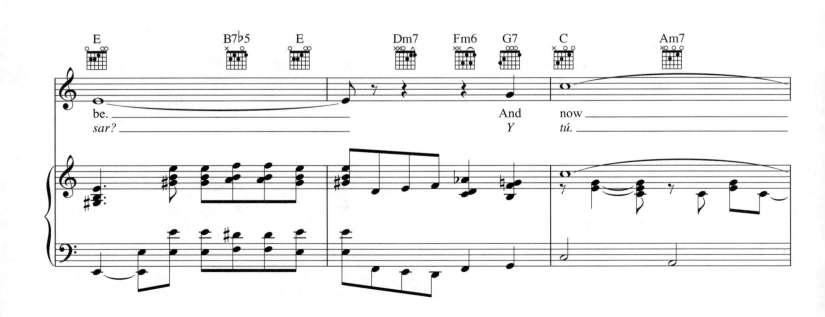

be. _____ And now _____
sar? _____ Y tú. _____

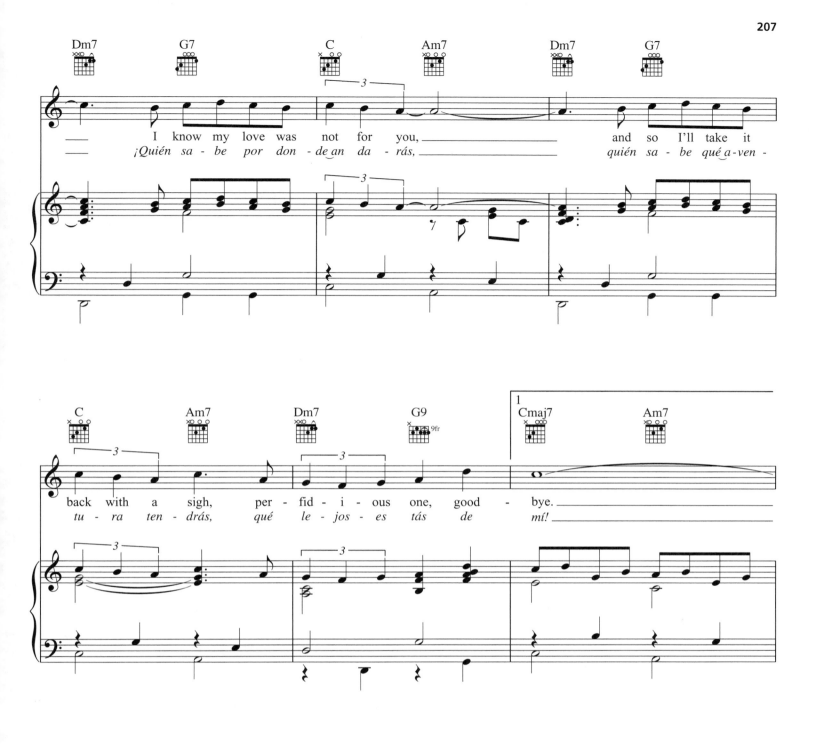

POINCIANA
(Song of the Tree)

Words by BUDDY BERNIER
Music by NAT SIMON

QUIET NIGHTS OF QUIET STARS
(Corcovado)

English Words by GENE LEES
Original Words and Music by ANTONIO CARLOS JOBIM

QUIZÁS, QUIZÁS, QUIZÁS
(PERHAPS, PERHAPS, PERHAPS)

Original Words and Music by
OSVALDO FARRES
English Words by JOE DAVIS

You won't ad-mit you love me, ___ and so, how am I
Siem-pre que te pre-gun - to ___ que cuan - do co-mo y

ev - er ___ to know? You al - ways tell me, ___ "Per -
don - de, ___ tu siem - pre nie res - pon - des ___ "qui -

SAMBA DE ORFEU

Words by ANTONIO MARIA
Music by LUIZ BONFA

SÓ DANÇO SAMBA
(Jazz 'n' Samba)

English Lyric by NORMAN GIMBEL
Original Text by VINICIUS DE MORAES
Music by ANTONIO CARLOS JOBIM

SLIGHTLY OUT OF TUNE
(Desafinado)

English Lyric by JON HENDRICKS and JESSIE CAVANAUGH
Original Text by NEWTON MENDONCA
Music by ANTONIO CARLOS JOBIM

Love is like a nev - er - end - ing mel - o - dy,___
Once your kiss - es raised me to a fe - ver pitch.___

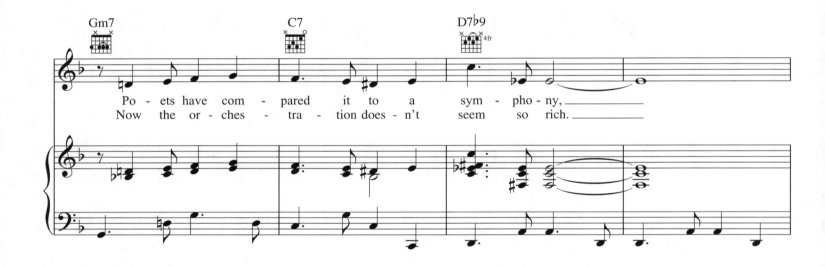

Po - ets have com - pared it to a sym - pho - ny,___
Now the or - ches - tra - tion does - n't seem so rich.___

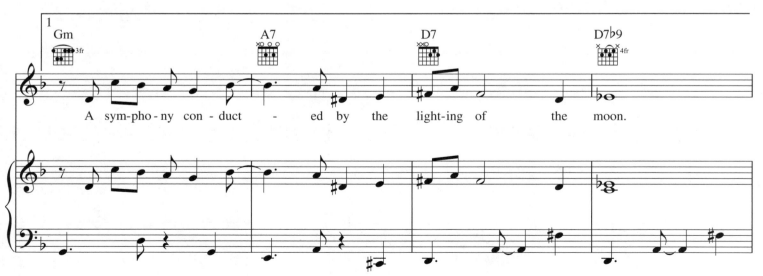

A sym - pho - ny con - duct - ed by the light - ing of the moon.

SO NICE
(Summer Samba)

Original Words and Music by MARCOS VALLE
and PAULO SERGIO VALLE
English Words by NORMAN GIMBEL

Relaxed Bossa Nova

Some-one to hold me tight, that would be ver - y nice, some-one to love me right,
that would be ver - y nice. Some-one to un-der-stand each lit - tle dream _ in me,
some-one to take my hand, to be a team _ with me. So nice, _____

SOMEONE TO LIGHT UP MY LIFE
(Se todos fossem iguais a você)

English Lyric by GENE LEES
Original Text by VINICIUS DE MORAES
Music by ANTONIO CARLOS JOBIM

Search - ing for some - thing or some - one to light up my life.
se to - dos fos - sem no mun - do i - guais a vo - cê.

life. _____
cê. _____

SPANISH EYES

Words by CHARLES SINGLETON and EDDIE SNYDER
Music by BERT KAEMPFERT

SWAY
(Quien será)

English Words by NORMAN GIMBEL
Spanish Words and Music by PABLO BELTRAN RUIZ

When ma-rim-ba rhy-thms start to play, dance with me,
make me sway.___ Like the la-zy o-cean hugs the shore,
hold me close, sway me more.___ Like a flow-er bend-ing

Quien se - rá la que me quie-ra a mi Quien se - rá
Quien se - rá___ Quien se - rá la que me dé su a-mor
Quien se - rá Quien se - rá___ Yo no sé si la po-

TICO TICO
(Tico tico no fuba)

Words and Music by ZEQUINHA ABREU,
ALOYSIO OLIVEIRA and ERVIN DRAKE

TICO TICO
As recorded by Herb Ohta Jr.
(From the 2001 Album 'UKULELE DREAM)

Generated using the Power Tab Editor by Brad Larsen. http://powertab.guitarnetwork.org

TICO TICO
(Tico no fuba)

Words and Music by ZEQUINHA ABREU,
ALOYSIO OLIVEIRA and ERVIN DRAKE

Bright samba

Oh Ti-co Ti-co tick! _ Oh Ti-co Ti-co tock! _ This Ti-co Ti-co he's the cuck-oo in my clock. And when he

says: "Cuck-oo!" _ he means it's time to woo; _ it's "Ti-co time" for all the lov-ers in the block. I've got a heav-y date _ a tête-à-

tête at eight, _ so speak, oh Ti-co, tell me is it get-ting late? If I'm on time: "Cuck-oo!" _ but if I'm late, "Woo - woo!" _ The one my

heart has gone to may not want to wait! For just a bir-die, and a bir-die who goes no-where, he knows of ev-'ry Lov-ers' Lane and how to

go there. For in af-fairs of the heart, _ my Ti-co's ter-ri-bly smart. _ He tells me: "Gent-ly sen-ti-ment-'ly at the start!" Oh-oh, I

hear my lit-tle Ti-co Ti-co call - ing, be-cause the time is right and shades of night are fall - ing. I love that

not-so-cuck-oo cuck-oo in the clock: Ti - co Ti - co Ti - co Ti - co Ti - co tock. tock.

Interlude

D.S. al Fine
(take 2nd ending)

TIME WAS

English Words by S.K. RUSSELL
Music by MIGUEL PRADO

TRISTE

By ANTONIO CARLOS JOBIM

Sad __ is to live in sol - i - tude __

far __ from your tran - quil al - ti - tude. __

Portuguese Lyrics

Triste é viver a na solidão
Na dor cruel de uma paixão
Triste é saber que ninguem pade viver de ilusão
Que nunca vai ser, nunca dar
O sonhador tem que acordar.

Tua beleze é um auião
Demals pra um pobre coracao
Ques para pra te ver passar
So pra se maltratar
Triste é viver na solidãd.

WATCH WHAT HAPPENS

from THE UMBRELLAS OF CHERBOURG

Music by MICHEL LEGRAND
Original French Text by JACQUES DEMY
English Lyrics by NORMAN GIMBEL

WAVE

Words and Music by
ANTONIO CARLOS JOBIM

Portuguese Lyrics

Vou te contar, os olhos já não podem ver,
Coisas que só o coração pode entender.
Fundamental é mesmo o amor,
É impossível ser feliz sozinho.

O resto é mar, é tudo que não sei contar.
São coisas lindas, que eu tenho pra te dar.
Vem de mansinho abrisa e mediz,
É impossível ser feliz sozinho.

Da primeira vez era a cidade,
Da segunda o cais e a eternidade.

Agora eu já sei, da onda que se ergueu no mar,
E das estrelas que esquecemos de contar.
O amor se deixa surpreender,
Enquanto a noite vem nos envolver.

WHAT A DIFF'RENCE A DAY MADE

English Words by STANLEY ADAMS
Music and Spanish Words by MARIA GREVER

YELLOW DAYS

English Lyric by ALAN BERNSTEIN
Music and Spanish Lyric by ALVARO CARRILLO

With an easy flow

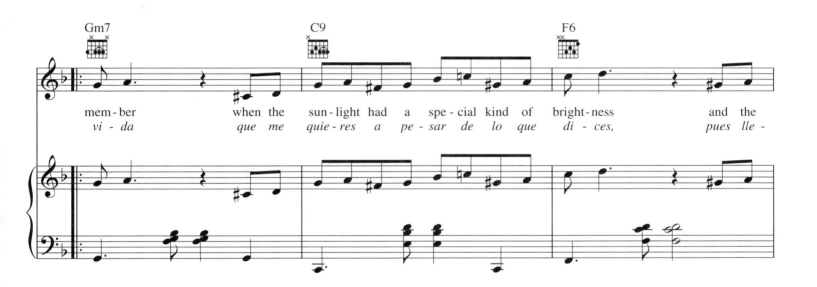

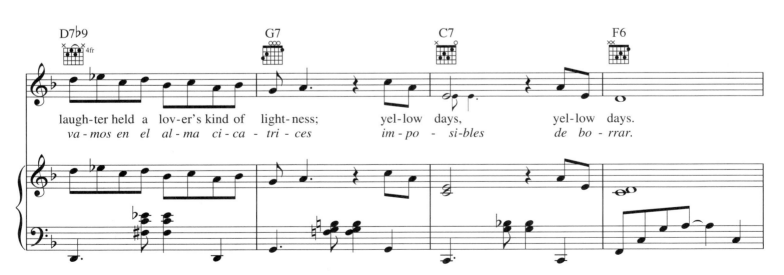

YOU BELONG TO MY HEART
(Solamente una vez)

Music and Spanish words by AGUSTÍN LARA
English Words by RAY GILBERT

THE BEST EVER COLLECTION

ARRANGED FOR PIANO, VOICE AND GUITAR

150 of the Most Beautiful Songs Ever
150 ballads: Bewitched • (They Long to Be) Close to You • How Deep Is Your Love • I'll Be Seeing You • Unchained Melody • Yesterday • Young at Heart • more.
00360735 ....$24.95

150 More of the Most Beautiful Songs Ever
More classics include: All I Ask of You • Can You Feel the Love Tonight • Change the World • Dream a Little Dream of Me • Imagine • Let's Fall in Love • Love Me Tender • and dozens more.
00311318 P/V/G $24.95

Best Acoustic Rock Songs Ever
65 acoustic hits: Dust in the Wind • Fast Car • I Will Remember You • Landslide • Leaving on a Jet Plane • Maggie May • Tears in Heaven • Yesterday • more.
00310984 ....$19.95

Best Big Band Songs Ever
Over 60 big band hits: Boogie Woogie Bugle Boy • Don't Get Around Much Anymore • In the Mood • Moonglow • Sentimental Journey • Who's Sorry Now • more.
00359129 ....$16.95

Best Broadway Songs Ever
Over 70 songs in all! Includes: All I Ask of You • Bess, You Is My Woman • Climb Ev'ry Mountain • Comedy Tonight • If I Were a Rich Man • Ol' Man River • more!
00309155 ....$24.95

Best Children's Songs Ever
Over 100 songs: Bingo • Eensy Weensy Spider • The Farmer in the Dell • On Top of Spaghetti • Puff the Magic Dragon • Twinkle, Twinkle Little Star • and more.
00310360 (Easy Piano) $19.95

Best Christmas Songs Ever
More than 60 holiday favorites: Frosty the Snow Man • A Holly Jolly Christmas • I'll Be Home for Christmas • Rudolph, The Red-Nosed Reindeer • Silver Bells • more.
00359130 ....$19.95

Best Classic Rock Songs Ever
Over 60 hits: American Woman • Bang a Gong • Cold As Ice • Heartache Tonight • Rock and Roll All Nite • Smoke on the Water • Wonderful Tonight • and more.
00310800 ....$19.95

Best Classical Music Ever
Over 80 of classical favorites: Ave Maria • Canon in D • Eine Kleine Nachtmusik • Für Elise • Lacrymosa • Ode to Joy • William Tell Overture • and many more.
00310674 (Piano Solo) $19.95

Best Contemporary Christian Songs Ever
Over 70 favorites, including: Awesome God • El Shaddai • Friends • Jesus Freak • People Need the Lord • Place in This World • Serve the Lord • Thy Word • more.
00310558 ....$19.95

Best Country Songs Ever
78 classic country hits: Always on My Mind • Crazy • Daddy Sang Bass • Forever and Ever, Amen • God Bless the U.S.A. • I Fall to Pieces • Through the Years • more.
00359135 ....$19.95

Best Early Rock 'n' Roll Songs Ever
Over 70 songs, including: Book of Love • Crying • Do Wah Diddy Diddy • Louie, Louie • Peggy Sue • Shout • Splish Splash • Stand By Me • Tequila • and more.
00310816 ....$17.95

Best Easy Listening Songs Ever
75 mellow favorites: (They Long to Be) Close to You • Every Breath You Take • How Am I Supposed to Live Without You • Unchained Melody • more.
00359193 ....$19.95

Best Gospel Songs Ever
80 gospel songs: Amazing Grace • Daddy Sang Bass • How Great Thou Art • I'll Fly Away • Just a Closer Walk with Thee • The Old Rugged Cross • more.
00310503 ....$19.95

Best Hymns Ever
118 hymns: Abide with Me • Every Time I Feel the Spirit • He Leadeth Me • I Love to Tell the Story • Were You There? • When I Survey the Wondrous Cross • and more.
00310774 ....$18.95

Best Jazz Standards Ever
77 jazz hits: April in Paris • Beyond the Sea • Don't Get Around Much Anymore • Misty • Satin Doll • So Nice (Summer Samba) • Unforgettable • and more.
00311641 ....$19.95

More of the Best Jazz Standards Ever
74 beloved jazz hits: Ain't Misbehavin' • Blue Skies • Come Fly with Me • Honeysuckle Rose • The Lady Is a Tramp • Moon River • My Funny Valentine • and more.
00311023 ....$19.95

Best Latin Songs Ever
67 songs: Besame Mucho (Kiss Me Much) • The Girl from Ipanema • Malaguena • Slightly Out of Tune (Desafinado) • Summer Samba (So Nice) • and more.
00310355 ....$19.95

Best Love Songs Ever
65 favorite love songs, including: Endless Love • Here and Now • Love Takes Time • Misty • My Funny Valentine • So in Love • You Needed Me • Your Song.
00359198 ....$19.95

Best Movie Songs Ever
74 songs from the movies: Almost Paradise • Chariots of Fire • My Heart Will Go On • Take My Breath Away • Unchained Melody • You'll Be in My Heart • more.
00310063 ....$19.95

Best Praise & Worship Songs Ever
80 all-time favorites: Awesome God • Breathe • Here I Am to Worship • I Could Sing of Your Love Forever • Open the Eyes of My Heart • Shout to the Lord • more.
00311057 ....$19.95

Best R&B Songs Ever
66 songs, including: Baby Love • Endless Love • Here and Now • I Will Survive • Saving All My Love for You • Stand By Me • What's Going On • and more.
00310184 ....$19.95

Best Rock Songs Ever
Over 60 songs: All Shook Up • Blue Suede Shoes • Born to Be Wild • Every Breath You Take • Free Bird • Hey Jude • We Got the Beat • Wild Thing • more!
00490424 ....$18.95

Best Songs Ever
Over 70 must-own classics: Edelweiss • Love Me Tender • Memory • My Funny Valentine • Tears in Heaven • Unforgettable • A Whole New World • and more.
00359224 ....$22.95

More of the Best Songs Ever
79 more favorites: April in Paris • Candle in the Wind • Endless Love • Misty • My Blue Heaven • My Heart Will Go On • Stella by Starlight • Witchcraft • more.
00310437 ....$19.95

Best Standards Ever, Vol. 1 (A-L)
72 beautiful ballads, including: All the Things You Are • Bewitched • God Bless' the Child • I've Got You Under My Skin • The Lady Is a Tramp • more.
00359231 ....$17.95

Best Soul Songs Ever
70 hits include: Cry Baby • Green Onions • I Got You (I Feel Good) • In the Midnight Hour • Knock on Wood • Let's Get It On • Mustang Sally • Respect • Soul Man • What's Going On • and dozens more.
00311427 ....$19.95

More of the Best Standards Ever, Vol. 1 (A-L)
76 all-time favorites: Ain't Misbehavin' • Always • Autumn in New York • Desafinado • Fever • Fly Me to the Moon • Georgia on My Mind • and more.
00310813 ....$17.95

Best Standards Ever, Vol. 2 (M-Z)
72 songs: Makin' Whoopee • Misty • My Funny Valentine • People Will Say We're in Love • Smoke Gets in Your Eyes • Strangers in the Night • Tuxedo Junction • more.
00359232 ....$17.95

More of the Best Standards Ever, Vol. 2 (M-Z)
75 more stunning standards: Mona Lisa • Mood Indigo • Moon River • Norwegian Wood • Route 66 • Sentimental Journey • Stella by Starlight • What'll I Do? • and more.
00310814 ....$17.95

Best Torch Songs Ever
70 sad and sultry favorites: All by Myself • Crazy • Fever • I Will Remember You • Misty • Stormy Weather (Keeps Rainin' All the Time) • Unchained Melody • and more.
00311027 ....$19.95

Best TV Songs Ever
Over 50 fun and catchy theme songs: The Addams Family • The Brady Bunch • Happy Days • Mission: Impossible • Where Everybody Knows Your Name • and more!
00311048 ....$17.95

Best Wedding Songs Ever
70 songs of love and commitment: All I Ask of You • Endless Love • The Lord's Prayer • My Heart Will Go On • Trumpet Voluntary • Wedding March • and more.
00311096 ....$19.95

FOR MORE INFORMATION, SEE YOUR LOCAL MUSIC DEALER, OR WRITE TO:

HAL•LEONARD™
CORPORATION

7777 W. BLUEMOUND RD. P.O. BOX 13819 MILWAUKEE, WI 53213

Visit us on-line for complete songlists at
www.halleonard.com

Prices, contents and availability subject to change without notice. Not all products available outside the U.S.A.

0308

This exciting series profiles the many styles of Latin music. Each folio contains 25 top hits from its specific genre for piano/vocal/guitar. Only $14.95 each!

¡PURA BACHATA!

Inviting collection of 25 love songs set to bachata, a highly popular rhythm from the Dominican Republic that features gentle percussion fills and tinkly guitar lines. Includes: Aquí Conmigo • Dos Locos • Tú Eres Ajena • Yo Sí Me Enamoré • Extraño A Mi Pueblo • Se Fue Mi Amor • and more.

00310946 Piano/Vocal/Guitar $14.95

¡PURO BRAZILIAN!

25 hits direct from Brazil, in both English and Portuguese! Includes: Agua De Beber • Aguas De Marco • Brazil • Chega De Saudade • Deixa • Desafinado • The Girl from Ipanema • Insensatez • Mas Que Nada • Meditacão • Amor Em Paz • Só Danço Samba • So Nice • Tristeza • Wave • and more.

00310976 Piano/Vocal/Guitar $14.95

¡PURA CUMBIA!

First-rate compendium spotlighting Colombia's famous lilting groove. 25 songs, including: La Pollera Colerá • Mete Y Saca • A Mi Dios Todo Le Debo • Tabaco Y Ron • Cumbia De Mi Tierra • Distancia • Guepaje • La Oaxaqueña • Luz De Cumbia • Maruja • Soledad • and more.

00310947 Piano/Vocal/Guitar $14.95

¡PURA SALSA!

A peerless collection of 25 salsa chestnuts, including: A Puro Dolor • Pena De Amor • Celos • Déjate Querer • No Morirá • Qué Hay De Malo • Si La Ves • Una Aventura • Cuando Faltas Tú • Micaela • Por Ese Hombre • Tu Recuerdo • and more.

00310949 Piano/Vocal/Guitar $14.95

¡PURO MERENGUE!

This foremost collection contains 25 sizzling fan favorites, including: Suavemente • Tu Sonrisa • Bajo La Lluvia • Pégame Tu Vício • Yo Te Confieso • Cuando Acaba El Placer • Bandida • Corazón De Mujer • El Tiburón • La Ventanita • Mi Reina • Niña Bonita • and more.

00310948 Piano/Vocal/Guitar $14.95

¡PURO MEXICANO!

Mexicano is not a specific genre, per se, but rather a broad musical classification that refers to the diverse categories of Mexican music, including banda, randera, cumbia, and grupera. This songbook gathers 17 Mexicano favorites, including: Amorcito Mío • Manantial De Llanto • No Me Se Rajar • Que Bonito Amor • Secreto De Amor • Te Solte La Rienda • Un Idiota • Un Sueño • and more.

00310972 Piano/Vocal/Guitar $14.95

¡PURO TEJANO!

Tejano evergreens by Los Kumbia Kings and Selena headline this exclusive set. 25 songs, including: SSHHH!!! • Amor Prohibido • Azúcar • Como Flor • Boom Boom • Fotos Y Recuerdos • Baila Esta Cumbia • Costumbres • Me Estoy Enamorando • Te Quiero A Tí • and more.

00310950 Piano/Vocal/Guitar $14.95

¡PURO VALLENATO!

Kinetic, accordion-powered classics from Colombia's Atlantic coast. 25 songs, including: Déjame Entrar • El Santo Cachón • Fruta Fresca • Alicia Adorada • No Pude Quitarte Las Espinas • Aquí Conmigo • Embrujo • Festival En Guararé • La Patillalera • Luna Nueva • Pedazo De Acordeón• Tierra Mala • and more.

00310951 Piano/Vocal/Guitar $14.95

Prices, contents, and availability subject to change without notice.

FOR MORE INFORMATION, SEE YOUR LOCAL MUSIC DEALER, OR WRITE TO:

HAL•LEONARD®
CORPORATION
7777 W. BLUEMOUND RD. P.O. BOX 13819 MILWAUKEE, WI 53213

Visit Hal Leonard online at www.halleonard.com

0904